Original title:
The Meaning of Life (Or Was It Lunch?)

Copyright © 2025 Creative Arts Management OÜ
All rights reserved.

Author: Evan Hawthorne
ISBN HARDBACK: 978-1-80566-188-7
ISBN PAPERBACK: 978-1-80566-483-3

Reflections Over Bread and Butter

Sitting here with toast so warm,
I ponder why I must conform.
Is butter spread on both sides fair?
Or should I ration calorie despair?

My coffee brews like thoughts collide,
Each sip a query, can't decide.
Do crumbs hold secrets of the great?
Or just attract the dogs I hate?

Morsels of Purpose

A sandwich crust can hold a dream,
But sometimes I just want ice cream.
Between the bites, I search for sense,
Is there wisdom in my past pretense?

Nibbles of joy, oh so divine,
While pondering if cheese is fine.
Could nachos lead to inner peace?
Or just a craving that won't cease?

Dining with Doubt

I scanned the menu, oh what a mess,
Is life just fries or something less?
Questions bubble like hot soup here,
Is there comfort after I disappear?

The cake looks tempting, but will it last?
I fear its sweetness holds my past.
Each bite a lesson, or just a tease?
Maybe life's just a string of these?

An Appetite for Answers

Grapes in hand, I ponder my fate,
Do snacks reveal more than a plate?
An apple a day, that's what they say,
But I nibble doubts that come my way.

Between bites I lose track of time,
Doughnuts and riddles, oh what a rhyme!
Is meaning found in dipping bread?
Or just more crumbs upon my head?

Culinary Contemplations

What's a carrot dressed in thyme?
Is it wisdom, or just snack time?
Lettuce pray for meaning deep,
While pizza dreams invade our sleep.

Forks and knives with thoughts so rare,
While casseroles hover in mid-air.
Spices whisper, secrets blend,
Is this the start, or just the end?

The Recipe for Understanding

In a pot, mix joy and doubt,
Simmer slowly, let it out.
A pinch of humor, dash of zest,
What's the final choice? A quest!

Sauté the urge to contemplate,
Chop the chaos, stir the fate.
Bake it lightly, cool it down,
Taste the joy; don't wear a frown!

Whispers in the Salad

Romaine lettuce spills its lore,
As croutons dance and bacon soars.
What is life? Just a veggie spree,
Or is it just a topping spree?

Dressing dreams on leafy greens,
Crunching thoughts, or so it seems.
With every bite, we lose and find,
Salad days, so intertwined!

Gastronomic Journeys

On a road paved with garlic bread,
Each crumb leaves thoughts in our head.
Steak out those queries, grill 'em right,
Are we just seasoning, lost in delight?

Breads tell tales of rise and fall,
In every bite, we have it all.
So savor now, don't let it go,
In this feast, wisdom may show!

Gluttony of Thoughts

Thoughts like pizza stacked high,
Toppings of doubts flying by.
I chew on dreams, a messy pie,
Crunch of wishes, oh me, oh my.

Should I have salad or fries?
Life's choices come with extra pies.
Calories count when fun complies,
Gluttonous brains eat the wise.

Hunger for Truth

Breakfast lies served with a grin,
Scrambled eggs of where you've been.
A side of bacon, truth's sly spin,
Devour knowledge, let's dig in.

Lunch arrives with a twist of fate,
Truth on a bun, can't hesitate.
Condiments of love on a plate,
Savory secrets, let's celebrate!

Cups of Coffee and Contemplation

Sipping thoughts like coffee hot,
Stirring dreams in a steaming pot.
A splash of cream, I think a lot,
Is this real? Or a caffeinated plot?

Espresso shots give me a buzz,
Whispers of wisdom with every fuzz.
Rising steam, like thoughts, it does,
In this cup, reality blurs.

The Lasting Taste of Temporal Transience

Time's meal served on a fleeting plate,
A gourmet dish but no debate.
Nibbling seconds, oh what a state,
Gone too soon; isn't that fate?

Desserts of moments flash and fade,
Sugar-coating, the games we played.
Each bite a memory, sweetly laid,
Life's buffet, we're all mislaid.

Bites of Bliss and Forks of Fate

A fork in life, which one to take?
Each bite we munch, a choice we make.
Savoring bliss, but for goodness' sake,
Don't choke on wisdom too hard to break.

Apricot dreams drizzled in light,
Feasts of laughter in the night.
Every morsel a quirky delight,
In this banquet, we take flight.

Salad Days and the Philosophy of Crunch

Lettuce in a quandary, who knew it would last?
Cucumbers pondering, memories of the past.
Tomatoes debate what's really divine,
In a bowl of greens, we search for a sign.

Carrots are dancing, but they won't tell why,
Dressing on the side, we give it a try.
Croutons are hopping, all crispy and bright,
Giving life lessons with every small bite.

Exchanges, Empathy, and Warm Dishes

At a potluck table, we gather and share,
Pastas are whispering, saying "Do you care?"
Chili's exchanging tales with warm bread,
Laughter in ladles, as love is widespread.

Beneath the casseroles, friendships ignite,
With each scoop of comfort, everything feels right.
Desserts join the party, oh what a delight,
Sprinkling sweetness, for futures so bright.

From Farm to Fork: Tasting Time's Lessons

The carrots are curious, asking for a taste,
As broccoli smiles, savoring not to waste.
Cornfields are chuckling, it's harvest time fun,
Nature's big buffet, for everyone!

Potatoes proclaim they have wisdom to share,
As garlic breathes stories of culinary flair.
From soil to skillet, each bite bears a tale,
In each crunchy moment, our thoughts never pale.

Beneath the Crunch, the Heartbeat of Being

Beneath the crispy shell, life has a spark,
Potato chips whisper secrets in the dark.
From popcorn's pop to the crunch of the crust,
Every tasty morsel holds wonders, we trust.

In every bite taken, there's laughter and cheer,
A quiche filled with wisdom, you need to hear.
As carrots crunch softly, they reveal what's true,
Life tastes amazing when shared with you.

Conversations Over Soup

In the pot, a mystery brews,
Chopped carrots share their views.
The broth giggles, the spoon sighs,
What's the secret? Soup replies:

Life's a slurp, a hearty taste,
A bowl of joy, no time to waste.
With every gulp, we seek to find,
The laughter brewed within the rind.

Crackers crunch with daring glee,
Dipping deep, we're fancy-free.
Each sip a quest, oh what a hoot,
As we ponder which came first, the fruit!

So let's toast with a spoon in hand,
To soup's lessons, oh so grand.
For in this broth, so rich, so bright,
We banter on 'til the soup takes flight!

The Enigma on the Plate

A salad whispers, 'What am I?'
Lettuce dreams of flying high.
With croutons laughing, nuts will sing,
As we ponder the meaning of everything.

Tomatoes wink, they know the deal,
Dressing drizzles with zestful zeal.
Forks clash in a battle of wits,
While beans debate their life amidst.

Potatoes stare, the mashed ones groan,
"Are we comfort food, or just alone?"
Onions chop, their tears in tow,
Finding answers hidden below.

Yet every bite is a puzzle piece,
In a world of flavors that never cease.
So let's dive in with a hungry grin,
For laughter's the spice where we begin.

Unraveled Napkin Philosophy

Naptime musings on fabric fine,
With spills of wisdom, red wine dine.
Crumbs of fortune, they flutter around,
As napkins ponder what truth is found.

Folded thoughts, a clever twist,
In every scrap, something missed.
Do we live to eat, or eat to thrive?
Such a tasty way to feel alive!

Our minds are like coffee, hot and brewed,
Caught in the drips of messy food.
Should ketchup reign, or mustard play?
A saucy debate to spice up the day.

So grab a fork, let's dig right in,
For life's a banquet with a side of grin.
And as the napkins flutter and sway,
We write our story in crumbs today.

Disheartened Desserts

Oh, cakes and pies in a sugary state,
Wondering why they don't get a date.
Whipped cream sighs, and chocolates pout,
"Is our purpose just to be eaten out?"

The brownies grumble, "We're misunderstood,
Just a sweet fix in a world that's good."
But ice cream melts, with a playful wink,
"Savor the moments, don't overthink!"

Tarts raise a fork, toasting their fate,
Chanting sweet hymns to celebrate.
Each cookie strolls with a crumbly cheer,
Laughing while savoring life's sheer veneer.

So here's to the desserts, let's feast with laughter,
For life's a treat, and joy's what we're after.
In every morsel, a giggle we find,
With sugar and spice, we toast to the kind!

Morsels of Memory on a Dimly Lit Table

On a table set with crumbs of cheer,
We ponder on things we hold dear.
Fork and knife like fateful tools,
Slice through moments, breaking rules.

A forkful of laughter, a dash of delight,
Savoring flavors that take flight.
In shadows cast by candle's glow,
We nibble on time, let it flow.

The coffee's strong, but so's the jest,
We spoon out stories, always a quest.
With each sip, a smile does bloom,
At this dimly lit table, we chase the gloom.

So raise your glass to the absurd,
Life's little joys, let's not defer.
Each moment a bite, every laugh a spread,
On this table of memories, we're well-fed.

Chopping Fates in the Kitchen of Existence

With knives in hand, we chop away,
Carrots and dreams on display.
A pinch of this, a sprinkle of that,
Stirring up laughter, imagine the chat.

In the pot of life, we toss our fears,
Simmering slowly with hearty cheers.
Fate gets diced, relationships sautéed,
As we cook up chaos, unafraid.

Whisking confusion into the mix,
A recipe's secret is quick-silver tricks.
Flavors collide, and plan goes astray,
But what's a dish without some play?

So here we stand, a wild brigade,
In this kitchen, let's never fade.
With laughter brewed and blunders galore,
Chopping fates? Oh, we want more!

Dining Outside the Lines of Destiny

On plates of fate, where rules are tossed,
We dine on dreams, never at a loss.
Spaghetti truths twirl in a mess,
Saucy moments we dare to confess.

Napkins tucked in, we're ready to feast,
On flavors of fortune, we're never least.
Doodles of joy on our tablecloth,
Messy and sweet, they show no wrath.

We raise a toast to the unknown,
With each clink, a seed is sown.
Outside the lines, we swirl and twine,
Dining on whims, we gladly dine.

Savor the chaos, embrace the bizarre,
For life's best moments are never too far.
With laughter and love, we're perfectly fine,
In this great banquet, we boldly shine.

Frenetic Flavors of Fleeting Moments

In the kitchen of time, things get wild,
With fleeting flavors, we're always a child.
Spicy memories, sweet pasts collide,
A buffet of moments, can't let them slide.

Chop, mix, and stir, as laughter erupts,
In this grand meal, life interrupts.
Each flavor's a giggle, each bite's a cheer,
Frenetic moments, we hold so dear.

Whisking wit into the dough of the day,
Bake it with sunshine, let it play.
The clock may tick, but we're not done,
In this feast of laughter, we've only begun.

So serve up the joy, let it bloom and expand,
With plates piled high, we take a stand.
Fleeting moments, like soufflés in flight,
In every bite, we find delight.

Cupcake Conundrums and Life's Icing

In a world of frosting, sweet and bright,
We ponder our flavors, day and night.
Are we red velvet or just a tease?
Life's a batch of cupcakes, if you please.

Sprinkles of joy, a cherry on top,
But watch out for crumbs, they never stop!
Is it chocolate or vanilla we crave?
Perhaps it's just frosting that we save.

With every bite, we're chewing through time,
Debating each choice, trying to rhyme.
Is this cake or a slice of fate?
Either way, we all might appreciate!

So laugh and enjoy this sugary ride,
For each cupcake holds secrets inside.
Life's light and fluffy, with layers to explore,
So take a big bite, and let out a roar!

Whisked Away by Whispers of Wonder

In the kitchen chaos, where spoons collide,
We whisk up our dreams, not always abide.
Are we soufflés, or do we just flop?
Every experiment could land us on top!

Baking with laughter, the oven's aglow,
Each cookie tells stories, as we bake and we flow.
Is it sugar that sweetens the days we forget?
Or is it just laughter at things we regret?

Whipped cream debates on who gets the last,
In this buffet of life, let's have a blast!
Are we just frosting? Or do we have zest?
A pinch of silliness adds to the quest!

Chasing the flavors, we dance and we sing,
In this crazy kitchen, oh, what joy we bring!
Life's a recipe crafted with fun,
So whisk away worries, and let laughter run!

Savoring Silence

In quiet moments, munching chips,
I ponder while the salsa drips.
Is life a feast or just a bite?
Crunching thoughts in endless night.

With some guac on the side, I muse,
Am I a chef or just confused?
A salad tossed with doubt and zest,
Each flavor fights to be the best.

The Snack Between Existence and Absurdity

Life teeters on a pizza crust,
Cheese and toppings, a must.
Do we choose toppings with great care,
Or let the grease just take us where?

In this buffet of silly fate,
Do I serve or do I wait?
My plate's a canvas, smear and spread,
With every bite, I dance instead.

Eternal Forks and Fickle Fates

I grabbed a fork to stake my claim,
But life flipped it; oh, what a game!
Spaghetti slurps, sauces fly,
Twisting noodles, oh my, oh my!

In this banquet of ups and downs,
I'm wearing smiles instead of crowns.
Fates roll dice, but here I stand,
With pasta dreams within my hand.

Whispers of Bread and Bliss

The toaster hums a soothing tune,
As butter melts to meet the swoon.
Is toast a sign of joy or pain?
I spread my thoughts like jam, insane.

In every crumb lies secret lore,
About the kitchen and much more.
Life might be just toast in the end,
But crispy edges can still transcend.

Pies of Potential and Crusts of Care

Life's like a pie, all sweet and round,
Slice it right, the joy is found.
But watch that crust, so flaky and bold,
Don't drop your dreams; they're precious as gold.

With every bite, a little surprise,
A cherry, a fortune, or maybe some lies.
Dig deep with a fork, let flavors collide,
In this goofy feast, take life in stride.

Gathering at the Table of Time

Gather round folks, the table is set,
With laughter and stories, there's no regret.
Pass the potatoes, but save me a roll,
In this banquet of hours, we fill up our soul.

The clock keeps ticking, but we just don't care,
With friends at our side, we breathe the fresh air.
So raise your glass, let the memories flow,
In this crazy dinner, we're all in the show.

Life's Buffet: Select with Caution

At life's grand buffet, be wary of greed,
For too much on your plate can cause quite a need.
Pick what you love and leave some behind,
Savor each bite, don't lose track of your mind.

A scoop of joy, a sprinkle of glee,
Watch out for the broccoli; it's not meant to be!
Cherry tomatoes are charmingly red,
Fill up on laughter; that's how we're fed.

Recipes for Resilience

A pinch of humor, a dash of cheer,
Mix it with heart, and chase off the fear.
Let simmer slowly, with kindness and style,
Serve it with gusto, and wear a big smile.

Ingredients vary; it's quite the affair,
Stirring in patience, show that you care.
Bake it all well in the oven of fate,
This recipe's wild, but it's never too late.

Plates of Perseverance

Stack up your plate with dreams and delight,
Even when life seems a troublesome bite.
Balance the flavors, both bitter and sweet,
With courage as dressing, you'll soon feel complete.

When the cheese starts to melt and the pasta's gone cold,
Remember the stories that time has told.
Add generous helpings and don't skip the fun,
In this banquet of living, we're all number one!

Existential Crumbs

In the fridge, the leftovers sleep,
While I ponder thoughts so deep.
Is it balance, or just some bread?
My sandwich dreams, they fill my head.

With mustard paths and pickle racks,
I seek the truth in culinary snacks.
Am I searching for the grand design?
Or just a slice of pizza divine?

A donut hole, what could it mean?
A portal to the unseen scene?
Doughy essence, sweet delight,
Makes me laugh through day and night.

But crumbs will fall, and spills will come,
As I muse on life's big drum.
Is happiness a bowl of soup?
Or just a snack for a foody loop?

A Feast of Questions

Why does pasta spiral and twist?
Is it fate or the chef's sweet wish?
What's the soup of the day, I muse?
A bowl of comfort, can't refuse!

Chasing flavors like hidden bounties,
Do we feast while pondering counties?
Salsa dancing on chips so bold,
Brings laughter in a world untold.

When dessert arrives, a cake so grand,
Do I, with fork, take a stand?
Is frosting wisdom dressed in cream?
Or just sugar in a dream?

Like forks and knives that never fit,
I wonder if life's just a silly skit.
Each bite's a riddle, each crumb a jest,
Eating in search of the ultimate quest!

Philosophical Leftovers

Left on my plate, what does it mean?
The cold rigatoni, a silent scene.
Do they whisper truths from days gone by?
Or just remind me to say goodbye?

In every wrap, a question waits,
Are we just meals on empty plates?
I ponder sauces and their tales,
While searching for wisdom in culinary trails.

Each sip of broth, a thought to chew,
Is it the answer, or just a stew?
Do we savor each bite, or rush ahead?
Like life, the feast must be well-fed.

So here I sit, my fork raised high,
Was the tart a joke, or just a pie?
With crumbs about, I'll take my stand,
Finding life in the food, ever so grand.

Nourishment for the Soul

If carrots are sticks, what grows inside?
A crunchy truth that one must confide?
Are beans philosophies, rich and complex?
Or just side dishes, time to perplex?

Lettuce debates with every leaf,
Seeking purpose beyond belief.
In every bite, a laugh or sigh,
Is this what makes our spirits fly?

The fries ask questions, hot and crisp,
"Were we meant to give life a whirl or a wisp?"
With ketchup dreams and tiny bets,
I contemplate culinary regrets.

So gather round, my friends and pals,
As we munch on truth, and giggles rouse.
Let's savor each morsel, each silly role,
For what's a feast without nourishing the soul?

Savory Secrets Lurking in the Pantry

In the cupboard, treasures hide,
Old spices, soup cans, oh what pride!
A box of noodles, a jar of jam,
Did I just find a three-legged ham?

Dusty jars of pickle brine,
Canned beans that once tasted fine.
Secret recipes, long forgotten,
Just add water? Or something rotten?

A bag of chips, now stale and gray,
Who was I feeding anyway?
Life's a mix of sweet and sour,
Even burnt toast has its power!

So dig in deep, uncover the loot,
What's molded could lead to a cute fruit!
Laugh at the snacks that look like crows,
In this pantry, anything goes!

Life's Menu: Choices and Consequences

A menu filled with lots of choices,
Each dish is served with tiny voices.
Pick the steak, or stick with fries,
Make a gaffe, and watch surprise!

Order sushi, but trust your gut,
Last time, it felt like a kitchen shut.
Dessert arrives, but oh the guilt,
Is it the cake, or the wish I'd wilt?

"Salad's good!" my conscience chimes,
Yet here I am, craving cheesy limes.
Life's just like that fancy meal,
Ordering thrills, just watch the keel!

Laugh at choices, let them dance,
Embrace the bloopers—what a chance!
For every bite that leaves a mark,
There's joy in flavor, a little spark!

Juicy Questions on an Icy Plate

On an icy plate, truth chills a bit,
Where's the ketchup? I must admit.
Why's life a roast, or ice cream cone?
Is it luncheon meat, or am I alone?

Ponder the burger, sizzle that cheese,
What's the side dish to moments like these?
Sipping soup while dreams take flight,
Are we just snacks in a starlit night?

Waiter, why's life served à la mode?
Questions pile up, it's quite the load.
Grab a fork, let's poke at fate,
Is this the path, or merely bait?

Laugh at the menu, flip through the fun,
Food for thought, it's never done!
With every bite in this grand debate,
Are we just lunch, or something great?

When the Soul Craves Sautéed Dreams

A soul that simmers in a pan,
Whispers of hopes; you've got a plan.
Sauté those dreams with garlic flair,
Toss in some laughter; no need to share!

Chop up regrets like old green beans,
Splash on some laughter, it redeems.
Season with joy, or is that zest?
A pinch of chaos is truly the best!

Stir-fry the fears, let them collide,
In this kitchen, there's nowhere to hide.
Serve on plates of bold design,
Feeding our souls, oh how divine!

So when life simmers, give it a whirl,
No recipe needed, just give it a twirl.
Harvest the flavors, both wild and tame,
In this sautéed dance, it's never the same!

A Tapestry of Tastes and Timelessness

In a café with buttered toast,
We ponder what matters the most.
Is it crumbs on your plate or a chat?
Or perhaps just a worry-free nap?

With coffee as deep as our thought,
Sips of wisdom that life has brought.
Forks dancing in laughter's embrace,
Every flavor finds its own place.

A bagel-life twist, perhaps a croissant,
Questions on toppings we so nonchalant.
Yet every bite tells a story bright,
And joy hides in mornings' warm light.

Could wisdom be found in a pie?
Or just a good laugh over fries?
Ingredients blend like dreams we chase,
In every meal, warmth finds its space.

Dining on Detours: Pathways to Purpose

We wandered through menus, a map by our side,
Chasing the flavors of every odd ride.
Who knew a hot dog could offer such cheer?
Or a slice of pizza could bring us near?

With salads that tease and desserts that allure,
Each dish is a riddle, and laughter's the cure.
Talk of the cosmos while slurping some noodles,
Finding great meaning in cozy food poodles.

As burgers stack high, so do our dreams,
In each savory bite, we plot and scheme.
Yet, the ketchup spills like our plans sometimes,
A comedic twist in our funny life rhymes.

So here's to detours, however absurd,
To kitchens and banter, each joke and each word.
For purpose tastes best when served with a laugh,
Let's toast to the journey, the glorious path.

Eating the Impermanent: A Delicate Balance

Life's just a buffet, or so it seems,
With seconds on laughter, and firsts on dreams.
The salad bar waits, piled high with regret,
Yet, a crumby croissant is the best of the set.

We nibble on moments, both sweet and quite sour,
A cookie that crumbles holds power, not dower.
With ice cream melting just like our plans,
We scoop up the chaos with messy hands.

A soufflé of whims, with a side of delight,
We dance to the kitchen rhythm each night.
So savor the fleeting, let flavors entwine,
In bites of the now, the future will shine.

Embrace every crumb, as the seconds will pass,
Each morsel a treasure, each laugh, like a class.
In this feast of the fleeting, we all take our stand,
To love while we dine, it's tasty and grand.

Soufflés of Sentiment in a Heavy World

In a world full of weight, we bake up some cheer,
With flaky regret and fond memories near.
A soufflé of laughter rises with care,
Whisking away woes, we lighten the air.

With each tasty morsel, we lighten the load,
A slice of perspective on this winding road.
The gristle of life, we chop into bits,
Each dish served with joy, a twist of wits.

As pickles disrupt our serious thought,
And donuts remind us of laughter we've sought.
A jamboree of flavors in a heavy dish,
Where bittersweet moments become what we wish.

So gather around for a grand potluck,
With sprinkles of joy, we'll change up our luck.
In soufflés of sentiment, the heart finds its glee,
In every shared bite, we find unity.

A Slice of Euphoria and a Dash of Despair

In the fridge of existence, I rummage through meats,
A leftover pizza, and life's little feats.
With each bite of joy, comes a side of regret,
Did I savor the moments or simply forget?

As I feast on my tacos, I ponder my fate,
Juggling my worries while munching on plate.
Life's little pleasures, like sprinkles of cheese,
Dance on my tongue with a hint of unease.

A salad of laughter, with croutons of stress,
Tossed with the vinaigrette of my daily mess.
Yet somehow I smile at this curious ride,
Slicing through sorrow, and taking it in stride.

In the kitchen of chaos, I cook up a dream,
Simmering thoughts while I whip up the cream.
With forks held high, we toast to the strife,
A slice of euphoria, a dash of this life!

Epicurious Journeys Across Cosmic Configurations

A journey of flavors, across stars and skies,
Where burgers and donuts bring cosmic surprise.
I bite into stardust, taste moonbeam delight,
With nachos of wisdom that glow in the night.

With each culinary step, I leave earth behind,
Exploring the galaxies, what treasures I find!
Celestial spices that twist in the air,
And gummy worm planets that float without care.

I dance with the comets, my plate full of dreams,
Galactic desserts with sugary beams.
Each orbit a meal, each blink a new treat,
Life is a buffet where laughter's the fleet.

Though gravity tugs me to the ground below,
I savor the journey; it's all quite a show!
From pasta-shaped planets to milky way pies,
Each cosmic bite shines, as my spirit flies.

Harvesting Happiness from Everyday Ingredients

In the garden of moments, I gather my glee,
Tomatoes of joy, planted carefully.
A sprinkle of laughter, a whisk of delight,
I bake up my dreams, all golden and bright.

With veggies of kindness, I sauté the day,
Infusing my heart with a warm, hearty ray.
Stir-frying troubles in olive oil bliss,
Every bite reminds me to savor and kiss.

Chopping up worries like a chef in a trance,
A dash of adventure, inviting the dance.
My recipe calls for a pinch of despair,
But sweetened with giggles, it's beyond compare.

So I feast on my harvest, from morning till night,
In every small moment, I find pure delight.
With each tasty morsel, I gather my song,
Finding happiness varied, amid what feels wrong.

Whimsical Whiskings through Celestial Food

With a whisk in my hand, I fly through the stars,
Mixing dreams in my bowl, a few galactic jars.
Baking cookies of wonder, with sprinkles of grace,
I whip up sweet giggles that ripple through space.

A cauldron of chaos, simmering lightly,
Stewing up laughter, it's bubbling brightly.
I toss in some whimsy, a dash of good cheer,
And serve up my magic, it's time to adhere.

Stirring galaxies round, in a cosmic contraption,
My culinary whims need no earthly caption.
With each cosmic sip, I savor the talk,
Tasting the joy in this whimsical walk.

For life's just a recipe, with flavors to blend,
So come take a bite, be my cosmic friend.
With each little taste, may you find your own groove,
In the kitchen of wonders, let's make our hearts move!

Forking Paths: Choices on a Silver Platter

In a café with choices galore,
I ponder if salad or dessert I adore.
My fork is confused, should it go left or right?
Each bite a dilemma, a comical plight.

Should I dare to risk the spicy Thai?
Or play it safe with a burger, oh my!
Each dish tells a story, both silly and sweet,
Yet tummy rumbles tell me it's time to eat.

The waiter's grin grows wider by the hour,
As I debate flavors with gastronomic power.
A sip of wine makes me contemplate,
If I'm living my best life or just on a plate.

Finally, I choose, triumphant with pride,
Life's just a menu and I'm the wild ride.
Forking my path with a wink and a cheer,
Let's order dessert! My purpose is clear!

Savoring the Silences Between Bites

In the quiet pause of a nibble so sweet,
Life's little treasures come out to greet.
Between each crunch, a giggle escapes,
As wisdom slips in like butter on grapes.

Laughter fills spaces where lettuce once lay,
I find my life's meaning in what chefs display.
Sauces of joy and salt of despair,
I savor the silence, with flavors to share.

Each chew is a journey, each swallow a tale,
What's profound in the bite of a melted cheese quail?
I ponder existence while feasting with friends,
Life's a buffet where absurdity bends.

So I lift my fork high in a toast to the day,
The silence between bites is my favorite way.
To laugh at the moments, both crumbly and sweet,
As I chase all my thoughts down a savory street.

Reflections in a Reflective Bowl

In a shiny bowl, my noodle thoughts swirl,
As I ponder if life's a microwave whirl.
With each twist of a fettuccine strand,
I contemplate choices, both daring and bland.

Shiny broth mirrors faces, some lost and some gleeful,
As giggles rise up, so silly yet real.
The aroma of garlic wafts thoughts into the air,
What's profound in the slurp of this noodle affair?

Dreams float like dumplings, soft and alive,
In this wacky world where flavors survive.
A sprinkle of laughs, a dash of delight,
Is life really serious? Oh, what a plight!

With each slurp, I ponder how to be whole,
If wisdom lies deep in this bubbling bowl.
So here's to reflections, both wry and sincere,
May the flavors be plenty, and laughter be near!

Gastronomic Journeys and Existential Feasts

On a quest for meaning, I chart my own course,
Through kitchens of wonder, I'll draw from the source.
I dip into dishes, from tacos to tarts,
Each plate tells a story, appealing to hearts.

As I munch on a mystery with noodles a-twist,
I realize existence may come with a twist.
With the crunch of a carrot, profound thoughts emerge,
Life's just a feast where we all love to splurge!

Gather round the table, my famished crew,
We'll share in these moments, both silly and true.
From appetizers bold to desserts that astound,
In every bite, meaning can be found.

So let's clink our glasses and savor this spread,
For life's just a banquet where nonsense is fed.
With each nibble and giggle, we chase the divine,
In culinary chaos, our souls intertwine.

Grains of Wisdom

In every crumb, a lesson hides,
Like breadcrumbs tossed on silly rides.
We gather thoughts, a feast to share,
While missing lunch, we munch on air.

We ponder life with fork in hand,
As salad dreams slip through the sand.
Is it the meal or the chat we crave?
Eating wisdom we try to save.

Fruits of Experience

Banana peels on paths we tread,
Life's fruity lessons, enough said.
Each juicy bite, a tale to tell,
Yet sometimes we slip and yell, "Oh well!"

The apples shine, but worms are near,
With every crunch, we face our fear.
Grapes of joy, they roll away,
In fruitcake dreams, we laugh and play.

Banquets of Being

At tables set with laughter loud,
Each guest a twist in life's own crowd.
With pudding, soup, and buttered bread,
We toast our whims and dance instead.

The main course comes with laughter's spice,
We chew on thoughts, oh, isn't it nice?
With every bite, we question fate,
Is this meal love, or just first-rate?

Dishes of Destiny on Wobbly Tables

The table shakes, the drinks will spill,
As destiny dances, what a thrill!
With every dish, a chance to sway,
Uncertain meals lead thoughts astray.

The cake's too tall, we laugh and cheer,
Will it fall down, or disappear?
Life's recipes from pots so bright,
We feast on chaos, sheer delight.

Nibbles of Notions

A crumb of thought, a tasty tease,
We snack on dreams, a bite with ease.
With every nibble, wisdom grows,
But sometimes we just chew on woes.

In morsels small, we find our way,
These witty bites brighten our day.
Life's a buffet, so take your pick,
You might just laugh until time's tick.

Pearls of Pudding

In bowls of cream, ideas float,
Each pearl a thought, a silly joke.
With sprinkles bright, we swirl and taste,
In dessert's delight, there's no time to waste.

Life's pudding pot may seem opaque,
But scoop with joy, for goodness' sake!
We share our spoons, and laughter rings,
In every bowl, a joy that clings.

Culinary Conundrums and Cosmic Queries

Do we savor each bite or search for the signs?
Are forks just for food or for probing divine?
Eggs on the plate, scrambled thoughts in the head,
Is breakfast the start, or is it all bread?

Pasta twirls dreams in a buttery dance,
While mustard whispers secrets—give ketchup a chance!
Do salads have feelings when tossed in a bowl?
Or is life just a snack, a mid-morning stroll?

Sipping soup, pondering, 'What's next on the list?'
Did we come for the meal, or did we just exist?
Gummy bears giggle, a sweet little bluff,
And macaroni wonders, "Is that really enough?"

At the end of the feast, when the dishes are done,
Did we munch on the truths or just have some fun?
With crumbs scattered wide and laughter's full bloom,
Was every bite wise, or just a sweet doom?

Appetites of the Soul: Myth or Meal?

Is pizza a treasure or simply a tease?
Can nachos enlighten amidst spicy cheese?
Grapes raise their voices, 'We're more than a snack!'
Do meals fill the void, or is that just a hack?

Cereal circles doubt if they're just round lies,
In the breakfast spectrum, do pancakes disguise?
Burgers, like philosophers, stack high with the truth,
While tater tots giggle, recalling their youth.

On toast, we lay wisdom, or is that just jam?
While quiche debates choices—"Am I prince or am?"
Are crumbs from the cookie the guide to our fate?
Or do they just hint that we should celebrate?

At brunch, we ponder if life's but a spread,
With mimosas deciding the paths we will tread.
Do coffee and cake hold the answers we seek?
Or is dessert just proof that we're all a bit bleak?

Sauces of Life, Spices of Existence

Is life just a sauce, tangy and bright?
Or a boring old paste that we mix just right?
Ketchup debates with the bold BBQ,
While garlic and herbs play the savory crew.

Sweet soy sauce whispers, 'What's life all about?'
Is it drizzle or drizzle, should we cringe or shout?
Olive oil glimmers with wisdom so fine,
While vinegar stings with weathered design.

A sprinkle of salt, are we all just a pinch?
Or a dash in the recipe, no cause for a wince?
Have thyme and nutmeg seen worlds full of strife?
Or do they just linger like dreams over rice?

In bowls filled with kindness, we savor the clay,
While sauces remind us that cooking's a play.
So stir up the pot, let flavors entwine,
For in every good meal, the humor's divine.

Dining with Dreams

At dinner, we ponder our hopes with delight,
While desserts dance around for the last little bite.
Do dreams taste like chocolate, or maybe they cake?
Or are they just filled with the choices we make?

Dining on wishes, with forks made of stars,
Do we toast to our visions with fries from the bars?
Glimpses of futures, like soup in a bowl,
Each flavor a glimpse of the parts of the whole.

Is dessert the finale, a cherry on top?
Or is it a moment before dreams take a drop?
Life's napkin humor is crumpled and smeared,
While appetizers laugh and tease all we feared.

So gather around for the feast of our dreams,
For laughter and joy are the best kind of themes.
With every course served, may we giggle and cheer,
For dining with dreams is the best meal, my dear!

Eating with Epiphanies

With every crisp bite, do we discover a clue?
Or is each revelation just something we chew?
Granola spills wisdom, the oats all agree,
That breakfast from packets can set your mind free.

Bite into tacos, and they whisper with zest,
'Are these crunchy truths, or is that just a jest?'
With guac on the side, can we find what we seek?
Or is that just the nachos playing hide and sneak?

While pudding cups ponder, 'Is this even a meal?'
Can desserts hold the secrets we're forced to conceal?
Ice cream has theories, but melts under the light,
While brownies demand, "Does your soul need a bite?"

So feast on these musings laid softly on plates,
For knowledge is tasty and oh so great rates.
With forks full of laughter, let's take one more chance,
To snack on the wonders of life's sweet romance.

Appetizing Ambiguities: Decoded

In a world of crumbs and dough,
We ponder why we're here, you know.
Is it for love or just a bite?
The answer wavers, always slight.

Salads tossed with dreams and fears,
We dress them up with laughs and cheers.
Each carrot stick, a life decision,
But vinaigrette smooths out suspicion.

Some seek fortune in the feast,
While others feast on thoughts released.
A slice of cake or maybe pie?
Just grab your fork and give it a try!

Between the meals, we munch on fate,
Unraveling truths that make us wait.
In every meal, there's joy and strife,
Like figuring out this thing called life.

Baking Expectations

Flour clouds and rising dreams,
We bake our hopes in golden beams.
A pie of wishes, round and sweet,
But watch your fingers, don't lose a beat!

Knead the dough of all your fears,
Add sugar, laughter, and some cheers.
For every rise, there's also fall,
Is it a cake or muffin, after all?

Whisking thoughts in a bowl so wide,
What's inside is hard to hide.
With icing dreams, we top it right,
Is it a pastry or a cosmic plight?

So take a bite of what you crave,
Life's oven waits, be bold and brave.
Whether sweet or savory delight,
When baked with love, it turns out right.

Taste Tests of Triumph

Sampling bites of joy and pain,
Every dish has much to gain.
A nibble here, a taste of strife,
All blend into this crazy life.

Testing flavors, some confuse,
With every lick, there's more to lose.
Is that despair or just a sprout?
Guess we'll find out when we chow out!

Sipping soup or munching bread,
Are we alive or just well-fed?
With every morsel, dreams take flight,
In each small taste, there's pure delight.

So fork in hand, let's take a chance,
In every bite, we find our dance.
With laughter seasoning every plate,
We live and feast; it's never late.

Spaghetti Strands of Connection

Twist and twirl of noodles long,
In every hug, the sauce is strong.
With a meatball or a dash of cheese,
Life's tangled threads can aim to please.

Al dente moments, firm yet true,
Running late, or finding you.
Each slurp tells a different tale,
In sticky sauce, we laugh and sail.

Spaghetti nights with friends abound,
In tangled pastas, love is found.
With garlic breath and hands entwined,
A plate of joy, our hearts aligned.

So let's dig in, and see what's there,
In every bite, a moment rare.
In this wild dish of love and strife,
We find the sauce, we call it life.

Licking Plates of Luminescence

Shiny plates, the remnants glow,
As laughter tickles, spirits flow.
Finishing bites, we wipe with glee,
Life's just a feast, come join and see!

Each leftover holds a story bright,
In every dab, there's pure delight.
With savory whispers, secrets shared,
In gleaming bowls, we're unprepared.

Dishes stacked with tales to tell,
In buttery bliss, we feel so well.
Licking plates, we seek the thrill,
In scraps of joy, we find our will.

So raise a glass, let's toast the day,
With goofy smiles, we drift away.
In every lick, a spark is born,
In tasty moments, life's reborn.

The Taste of Being

In the fridge of existence, we search and we peek,
What's for dinner? Or is it all bleak?
A slice of the cosmos, a forkful of fate,
With sprinkles of chaos on a large dinner plate.

Each morsel a moment, each sip a sweet breath,
Chasing the flavors, as life hints at death.
Do we savor the dish, or just fill our plate?
What's the recipe? Oh, I'm just fashionably late!

An omelet of dreams with a side of regret,
Life's a buffet; get what you can get!
But watch for the food fights, they come out of nowhere,
As ketchup and mustard float in the air!

So chow down on joy, sprinkle laughter with cheer,
For all of this feasting is finite, I fear.
With each bite of wonder, we dance with delight,
And hope that dessert doesn't give us a fright!

Meals and Musings

At breakfast, I ponder the toast and the jam,
If calories count, then who gives a damn?
The egg rolled on in with a great sense of flair,
Saying, "Scramble your thoughts; it's a culinary affair!"

For lunch, I devour my dreams with a side,
Of crispy reflections; they crunch with pride.
While salad sits sulking, like thoughts on the fence,
Saying, "Life's not so leafy, it just makes no sense!"

Dinner's a banquet of positive vibes,
We feast on our musings, like pies full of bribes.
Each nibble a question, each gulp a new thought,
As flavors unite in a savory plot.

With dessert comes the laughter, a swirl of delight,
Chocolate-covered wisdom, oh, what a sight!
So pass me the laughter, and let's toast to the night,
Life's a meal worth sharing, it's all so outright!

Spoonfuls of Introspection

With a spoon in my hand, I dig deep inside,
To uncover the secrets that I often hide.
Each scoop is a moment, each bite something new,
A taste of my being, with a sprinkle of blue.

Sipping on thoughts like a warm cup of tea,
Am I simply lost, or just being me?
The broth is confusing, yet savory too,
Do we sip to discover, or sip just to stew?

From noodles of worries to veggies of cheer,
Life's soup is a mix, whether far or near.
But watch for surprises; they float in the mix,
Like peas or like wisdom, we munch on the tricks!

So let's raise our bowls to the great unknown,
Each spoonful a journey, never alone.
For together we slurp through this whimsical stew,
And laugh at the flavors that blend into you!

Appetizers of Ambiguity

From finger foods signaling, I take a small bite,
Is it food or a metaphor? Left or right?
Each dip in the sauce, a perplexing cheer,
Do nachos taste better when shared with a peer?

Oh, the platter of choices is piled so high,
With wings of confusion that flutter and fly.
Shall I munch on my doubts or crunch on my fears?
Each crunch brings a giggle, dissolving my tears.

With every small nibble, I ponder and muse,
Are we snacking on life, or just tasting the blues?
Sliders of sanity, and salsa that sings,
My plate is a canvas; I paint with my wings!

So let's toast with our forks, and clink dishes with zest,
For dining on questions can be quite the quest.
With each scrumptious bite, let's embrace the unknown,
As appetizers jiggle, and we laugh while we've grown!

Beyond the Table: A Thought

In the lunchroom of destiny, we dine,
Plates piled high with dreams, a fine line.
Forks and spoons all clatter and clash,
Could purpose be just a well-cooked hash?

We twirl spaghetti, pondering fate,
Stuffing ourselves on the choice of our plate.
What if life's sauce is just a bad blend?
Or maybe it's just a snack in the end?

With chips and dip, we gather round,
As laughter's the secret flavor we've found.
Is wisdom hidden in crispy crumbs?
Or simply where the dessert life comes?

So let's raise a toast with a soda can,
To the pizzas of life—oh, what a plan!
When pondering worries, let's take a bite,
And laugh at the absurd, 'cause everything's right!

Lifelike Nourishment

In gardens of thought where we harvest delight,
The seeds that we plant grow both day and night.
Is the fruit we imagine more savory than bread?
Or just yesterday's leftovers, now cold and dead?

We snack on our wishes, a bite here, a chew,
Is that why we're hungry for something brand new?
Salads of dreams tossed in dressing of time,
But who knew existence could taste so sublime?

With each crunch we ponder the great cosmic meal,
Is it just snack-time or are we meant to feel?
As we share cheese sticks of laughter and fun,
Life's a potluck, and we all get a bun.

So pass me the chips and let's dip in the guac,
For meaning might just be a savory clock.
Fun friends and good food—what more could you need?
Life's a buffet, so let's all take heed!

Chew on This: A Prelude

What if existence is just a café?
Where we order our dreams, but they serve dismay?
We sip on the soup of anxiety steeped,
While burgers of wisdom leave us all creamed.

Life's like a sandwich, stacked high with surprise,
One bite of the journey, then switch to fries.
But when we dig in, is it more than a snack?
Are we munching on moments, or just some good crack?

In the breakfast of choices, the pancakes stack high,
With syrupy sweetness, we might just fly.
But watch out for eggs that bring chaos and mess,
In the kitchen of life, don't settle for less.

As the clock strikes noon, let's gather and feast,\nOn
laughter and joy, we'll have our heart's least.
So munch on the magic that fills up the air,
In every great bite, know we're meant to share!

The Hidden Course of Existence

High in the pantry, in boxes so tight,
Are the snacks of the cosmos, all bringing delight.
Is the pie chart of life just dessert gone awry?
Or a buffet of moments that soar and fly?

Between morsels of laughter, we find our own path,
Unraveling riddles like a great math bath.
The soup of uncertainty thick as it steams,
Might just hold the recipe for all of our dreams.

As forks fight for freedom on a crowded plate,
We debate over onions, and what makes us great.
Is salad a dream or a cruel joke instead?
Do we really take risks, or just go back to bed?

So here's to the diners who laugh at the plight,
While feasting on questions that take us to flight.
In every small bite, let's discover our song,
For life is a feast, and together we belong!

Servings of Solitude in Crowded Rooms

In a room full of chatter, I nibble alone,
Lost in my thoughts with a sigh and a groan.
Everyone's munching, but I just sip air,
Feeling like a ghost in my own comfy chair.

Strangers are laughing, their joy fills the space,
But I'm over here, just in a noodle race.
My pasta's gone cold, but my heart's feeling warm,
What's on my plate? Just confusion in form.

They toast with their glasses, I toast to my fate,
I ponder my blessings while they celebrate.
A buffet of wisdom, a banquet of chance,
I'm dancing with solitude, in awkward romance.

Oh, the irony dwells in this feast full of cheer,
Amidst all the laughter, no one's drawing near.
So I chuckle aloud at the irony's bite,
My table's a realm where I'm king for the night.

A Feast of Questions Afloat on the Sea

Sailing on waves of uncertainty deep,
Questions like fish, in my mind they creep.
Do I savor the joy or just choke on the doubt?
Is the ocean my home or a giant takeout?

Floating on cruisers of hope and despair,
Do the seagulls judge me, or do they just stare?
Tossing the bread as my thoughts drift away,
What's better, a sandwich or existential play?

Riding the currents of "what if" and "why,"
Salt on my skin as the seagulls all fly.
Do they know my heart or just want my fries?
A boat filled with queries, oh how time flies!

So I laugh at the wave that just splashed on my face,
Questions may swirl, but my heart finds its place.
With a wink to the sea, I raise my glass high,
To the feast of confusion, let's all eat pie!

Buttered Choices and Creamed Conflicts

On toast with my doubts, I spread all my fears,
A drizzle of laughter, a sprinkle of tears.
Life's breakfast is tangled, with options galore,
Should I scramble my thoughts or just fry them some more?

With butter on choices and jam on the side,
Each bite is confusion, but I take it in stride.
Should I savor more sweetness or just skip the cake?
Pour syrup on truth, or is that a mistake?

Creamed conflicts arise, like a soufflé that's fallen,
Amidst all the chaos, I hear a soft calling.
Maybe it's brunch, or just dinner gone wrong,
In the kitchen of laughter, I know I belong.

So I whip up a smile, add spice to my chat,
Each morsel of life is a whimsical spat.
With each forkful of joy and a side of regret,
Let's feast on this madness—no need for a vet!

Reflections in a Frosty Glass

I gaze at my drink, wrapped in chilly embrace,
The ice clinks like laughter; it's a merry place.
What's swirling in there? My dreams or my gin?
Or a spicy dilemma that's brewing within?

As bubbles arise in my frosted delight,
Questions keep popping, like stars in the night.
Is that the truth inside, or just fizzy air?
Each sip turns to giggles, each gulp is a dare.

The reflection stares back, a comical sight,
Am I wise or just tipsy in this dim light?
A toast to confusion, a hiccup for zest,
In a world full of choices, a drink's just the best.

So let's raise our glasses, clink loud and clear,
In the end, what matters? Just the joy we can cheer.
Through shimmer and sparkle, we sip and we laugh,
Finding meaning in bubbles, or maybe just half.

Celestial Snacks on Cosmic Plates

In the galaxy's vast buffet,
Planets spin, searching for gourmet.
Asteroids toss, a crunchy delight,
Nibbling stardust, oh what a sight!

Nebulae swirl like cotton candy,
Distant suns shine, oh so dandy.
Cosmic fries, with a pinch of stars,
Galactic kitchens have no bars!

Martian muffins, a crumbly treat,
Jupiter's pie, quite hard to beat.
Comets pour milk over cereal bowls,
In this menu, there are no roles!

A taste of humor in every bite,
Universe giggles, what a delight!
Space chefs juggling, it's quite a show,
In this cosmic feast, we laugh and glow!

Philosophies Served with a Side

Wisdom fries with a tangy jest,
What's the point? Just take a rest!
Smiles blended in a shake of fate,
Sipping thoughts on a well-earned plate.

Pondering life, or maybe a snack?
To find the truth, you might need a nap.
Tacos wrapped in paradox dreams,
Filling our brains with silly themes.

On the menu, doubts stir and weave,
A side of laughter, we all believe.
Filet of reason, well-cooked but rare,
In this diner, we simply share.

Philosophers roast over boiling tea,
Chatting softly 'bout how to be free.
With giggles and bites, we munch and ponder,
Life's just a buffet, let's twirl and wander!

Crumbs of Existence

Life's just crumbs on a giant plate,
Tiny bits for a hefty weight.
Each little morsel serves a tale,
With laughter sprinkles, it can't fail!

From crusty bread to flaky pie,
Existence flutters, oh me, oh my!
Nibble on thoughts like cookies warm,
A lighthearted break, far from the norm.

Sprinkles of joy, a pinch of doubt,
Finding flavor in what it's about.
In the bakery of cosmic dance,
We share a laugh, take a chance!

So gather the crumbs, don't let them go,
Each little piece adds to the flow.
In the end, it's not what we eat,
But the joy we share, that's the real treat!

Bites of Truth

Truth bites are small but pack a punch,
Savory snacks in a lively lunch.
Morsels of wisdom, crispy and bold,
Wrapped in humor, never too old.

A slice of truth and a funny jest,
In every bite, a flavor quest.
Digging deep into the cosmic stew,
Each little nibble reveals something new.

Potato chips of clever minds,
Crunch away doubts that one finds.
With every taste, we giggle and chew,
Discovering secrets in every view.

So don't just munch, take a big bite!
Life's tasty morsels bring sheer delight.
With laughter alongside each tiny cheer,
The truth is savory, so have no fear!

Luncheon Lessons

At the lunch table, wisdom unfolds,
Between bites, the truth it holds.
Sipping soup with a dash of glee,
Sharing secrets, just you and me.

Lessons served with a side of fries,
Laughter bubbles; oh, how time flies!
Mixing flavors, we venture and roam,
In this bustling cafeteria, we find home.

Cheesecake talks after salad's task,
Life's strange route, our questions ask.
With every forkful, stories emerge,
In this grand diner, we freely purge.

So grab your napkin, let's take a seat,
In this humorous match, we can't be beat.
With every lesson, let's raise a toast,
To the laughter we share, we love it the most!

Afternoon Delights

Around the table, chatter and cheer,
Afternoon snacks bring us near.
Cookies and cream, laughter mixes fast,
Each bite we take, memories cast.

Giggling softly over sweet tea,
What's the secret? Just let it be!
Life's a circus, with cream puffs galore,
At this gathering, who could ask for more?

In every nibble, a silly tale,
Pastries flake, but we won't fail.
We gather crumbs like golden treasure,
Afternoon delights bring endless pleasure.

So munch away and soak in the fun,
In this bright moment, we're all one.
For life's a treat, we'll share and savor,
In a joyful feast, find all the flavor!

Scraps of Significance

Leftover thoughts, a plate in hand,
Wisdom crumbles, like stale bread,
We seek the truth in each bite we take,
But ketchup smears, and fries are dead.

Forks and knives, a dance so grand,
Chopping carrots of hope ahead,
But every question starts to blend,
Into a stew of what was said.

Cereal talks, milk spills allure,
Breakfast with metaphors galore,
Do spoons contain a secret pact,
Or just the crunch from life's décor?

Nibble lightly on wisdom's crust,
Or dive in deep, with fervor and zest,
In finding spice, we might just find,
That laughter's the flavor we like best.

Forking Paths

Two roads diverged, what a surprise,
One leads to cake, the other, fries,
Whichever way, the choice is tough,
Do I want sweet, or should I be rough?

Each step I take, with fork in hand,
Creates a fable, perfectly planned,
Do pickles have wisdom to share?
Or just crunch loudly without a care?

Chili or soup? The options abound,
I toss a coin, let the luck be found,
With every choice, a laugh we make,
Who knew life's wisdom was just a bake?

So gather 'round, let's share the dish,
Of silly thoughts and a marshmallow wish,
In this buffet of jests and fun,
We're all just diners, each and every one.

The Banquet of Existence

Gather 'round for a feast of thought,
With mashed potatoes, lessons are brought,
Rolls of humor, buttered with grace,
We fill our plates in this merry space.

Vegetables chatter, the dessert's a blast,
Conversations sweet, no topic is vast,
Cake layers whisper of dreams yet to chew,
Each slice a giggle, each frosting a clue.

In this grand hall, with friends so dear,
We toast to notions, to quirkiness, cheer,
For every laugh and crumb that we make,
Is a memory baked in our joyful cake.

So raise your glass, let's toast tonight,
To snacks of wisdom and laughter so bright,
In this banquet of giggles, we find our way,
With every nibble, we savor the play.

Chewing on Fate

Gum on my shoe, fate can be sticky,
I chew on choices, they're often tricky,
With each bubble popped, I ponder and sigh,
Is life a meal, or just what we spy?

Nibbling on dreams, I take a big bite,
What flavors await, in the day or the night?
Do cookies hold secrets, or just crumbs of fate?
I dive into snacks, yet ponder and wait.

Life's a buffet, with options galore,
Do I munch on wisdom, or pine for more?
Chomp through the chaos, enjoy the surprise,
With each crunch and giggle, my spirit will rise.

So here's to the grapes of potential we tread,
As I chew on my choices, I laugh 'til I'm red,
For who needs the answers when snacks are divine,
In the end, it's the fun that makes it all fine.

The Quest for Flavorful Purpose

In a world of endless dishes,
I seek the zest of bliss.
Each bite a quest for laughter,
With humor as my compass.

Pickles dance upon my plate,
Bouncing with a crunch so grand.
What's the point? Or just a snack?
Let's laugh and raise our hands!

Fries whisper secrets sweet,
While ketchup pools like dreams.
Am I here for joy, or fries?
Maybe both, it seems!

So I chase these flavors bright,
With giggles on my mind.
In every bite, a twist of fate,
Each morsel, pure and blind.

Salads of Serenity

In fields of greens, I ponder,
What makes a salad great?
Crisp lettuce or sweet tomatoes,
Ah, the choices are first-rate!

Croutons jumping in delight,
Bouncing off the lettuce leaves.
Am I tasting joy or just
The crunch that never leaves?

Dressing terms like 'whimsical',
Pouring hopes on all that's crisp.
Is this my Zen, a veggie cure,
Or a hungry munching lisp?

So I mix with joyful flair,
To find peace in every bite.
But as the bowls empty out,
I wonder if my heart feels light.

Soups of Sorrow

A bowl of broth, so warm and deep,
I stir my thoughts like stew.
Do onions cry in silence here,
Or is it just my view?

Peas floating like lost dreams,
Carrots shaped like fleeting time.
As I sip this liquid haze,
Life's riddles start to rhyme.

Bread crumbles tap dance around,
While spoons create their song.
Am I sipping life's regrets,
Or just where I belong?

With each slurp, a chuckle blooms,
For warmth sits in my lap.
In sorrow's broth, I taste the truth,
And giggle at the flap.

Morsels of Meaning Beneath the Surface

In pies where secrets lie,
I slice a piece of fate.
Is there wisdom in this crust,
Or just a slice that's great?

Cherries wink beneath the glaze,
As crumbs dance in delight.
Is life a pastry, sweet and grand,
Or just a late-night bite?

Beneath the layers, truths reside,
Some sweet and some quite sour.
But with each forkful, laughter grows,
In this edible flower.

So when your plate is filled with cheer,
Dig deep, don't shy away.
For in each morsel's fleeting crunch,
You might just find your way.

In Search of Nourishment and Insight

With a fork in one hand, I embark,
To elude the empty plate.
Is wisdom found in golden fries,
Or in salad whispering fate?

A taco sings of worldly truths,
As spices tingle my tongue.
Do I find enlightenment here,
Or just a meal to be sung?

Rice bowls whisper lessons hushed,
As I savor each warm grain.
Is life's essence in the sauce,
Or the joy that we gain?

So I journey through these bites,
With laughter as my guide.
For in the meals close to my heart,
I find comfort, fun, and pride.

Recipes of Reflection

In a pot of thought, let's stew,
Add a dash of laughter too.
Simmer gently, stir with glee,
Is it insight, or just a recipe?

Sprinkle in some curious spice,
What's the flavor? Once or twice!
Taste-test dreams that rise and swell,
Or was that just last week's swell?

A pinch of chaos, don't be shy,
Shake it up, let flavors fly.
Slice of time, a chunk of fun,
Chopped and served, who's second run?

Whisk together, let's not be tame,
Here's to life and food's fair game!
If the meal is bland or zany,
Who knew growth could taste so grainy?

Ingredients of Inquiry

What goes in this melting pot?
Questions bubble, quite the plot!
Shredded dreams and saucy schemes,
Cooked with hope's peculiar beams.

Peel the layers, dig right in,
Is there sweet where sour's been?
Mix it up, don't shy away,
Taste the truth, don't need to play.

Sprout some doubts, toss in a line,
The recipe's yours, some might whine.
Serve it hot, don't let it simmer,
Someone's fate? Or just a dinner?

Bake the questions, oh so bright,
Here's to pondering through the night!
Put on the oven glove of fate,
As we dish, we contemplate.

Tables Encircled by the Unknown

Gather 'round this wobbly table,
Sharing thoughts as best as able.
The chairs all squeak, the laughter roars,
What's for dinner? Who keeps score?

Mysteries served on a platter,
Chow down hard, let's make it matter!
Is it physics, art, or toast?
Raise your glass, we must all boast!

Inquiries dance amid the eats,
Spilling secrets like falling sweets.
What is life? The peas just roll,
As we dip and dive—what's the goal?

Yet laughter cradles every bite,
In this feast of day and night.
So let's keep munching, what's the fun?
Until the meal releases sun!

Eclipsing Plates Under Starry Nights

Under stars, the plates get stacked,
What's the truth? The mysteries packed!
Glimmers shine in the midnight glee,
As we serve up philosophy.

Bread so crusty, thoughts so light,
Nibble slowly, it feels just right.
A bite of ponder, a sip of laugh,
Is this the cosmos or just a calf?

Mix celestial pies with cosmic cheese,
Fleeting moments nestled with ease.
The night may whisper mock and tease,
What's the answer? Pass the peas!

So toast the stars, and let them guide,
In the kitchen where dreams collide.
Each recipe has its own delight,
In laughter's glow, we claim the night.

Ingredients of Gratitude

A sprinkle of thanks on every plate,
Let's savor seconds, don't be late!
Boil the love then serve it warm,
Who knew kindness could take form?

Garnish meals with your best cheer,
The laughter shares what we hold dear.
Steep the memories, rich and bold,
In moments treasured, joy unfolds.

Celebrate the clatter and the mess,
In every nibble, find the zest.
Forks and spoons in joyful flight,
Gratitude turns each bite so bright.

So gather round this hearty stew,
Thank the cook, for me and you!
Life's a feast, all dishes show,
In ingredients shared, we grow.

Flavors of Fear

Lurking shadows on the plate,
What's that lurking? Count your fate!
A pinch of dread, a slice of doubt,
Can we taste what life's about?

Sour notes in a jazzy tune,
Is fear a dish we eat too soon?
Serve it raw, let's face the scare,
But oh, the brave move on with flair.

Bitter chocolate, but sweet we find,
In every crunch, life's intertwined.
Maybe fears can be re-spiced,
Fried in courage, oh so nice!

So with each bite, we learn and grow,
The flavors shift, yet still we flow.
What's to fear on a dinner plate?
Perhaps it's just a twist of fate?

www.ingramcontent.com/pod-product-compliance
Lightning Source LLC
Chambersburg PA
CBHW051701160426
43209CB00004B/985